WHAT THE LIFEGUARD SAW

The Collected Poetry of

Will Schneider

ISBN: 978-93-90601-46-2

First Edition: 2022
Rs. 200/-

Cyberwit.net
HIG 45 Kaushambi Kunj, Kalindipuram
Allahabad - 211011 (U.P.) India
http://www.cyberwit.net
Tel: +(91) 9415091004
E-mail: info@cyberwit.net

Printed at Repro India Limited.

Artist Statement

As a writer, filmmaker, and poet, my work showcases the way I see and interact with the world around me. I often describe my art as being dictated by the statement, "the Devil and God are raging inside me." This does not necessarily mean I'm devoutly religious, rather it means that my creative pieces demonstrate the two sides of myself fighting for control: the angel and the demon, the lover and the hater, the optimist and the pessimist.

The "Devil" inside me is the one responsible for the dark side of my work. The violent horror films, the nihilistic stories about how empty life can be, and the bleak poems encouraging dread all fall under this umbrella. I have long been fascinated with the grey side of humanity and the problem of evil, and exploring this in my work has helped me cope with the idea that life is not perfect and never will be. Pretending it is does not benefit anyone, especially me.

The "God" inside me is the one responsible for the lighter side of my work. The hopelessly romantic films, the optimistic stories about how incredible human interaction can be, and the poems longing for an eventual soulmate all fall under this umbrella. While I know life is not perfect and I have to acknowledge that, there is also so much beauty in the world that it would be foolish to ignore. Nothing is ever fully good or bad.

I have been told that my writing and film work exercises a passion for human empathy and the mundanity of life that other creatives don't understand, and I work hard to make sure I capture honesty above all else. To quote one peer of mine, I "scrape the bottom so well." Meaning that I highlight simple, everyday people in a way few others possibly could. It's the best compliment I've ever received.

I often say that my work is not about characters who are "happy, well-adjusted people." It is about flawed humans in search of what they think will bring happiness. Whether the Devil or God is at their steering wheel, however, will always dictate what happens next.

Contents

BURIED HERE LIES ME

Now time stands still and so do I.

Here I've forgotten how to die.

My casket drops and I wonder,

How breath tastes at six feet under.

My neighbors are spiders and worms.

Ate myself, now they get their turns.

All is black yet it's clear to me,

Here alone, I can finally see.

FULL DAYLIGHT

He had often noted
that lifeguards only
realize you couldn't
swim long after you've
already drowned.
But this was the
exception. The anchor
he had fixed
to his feet for
so long ended up
a buoy. There
he was, on the
beach and breathing.
The sun was
his now.
No waves would
ever carry him
away again.

LIZ'S SONG

"And who would just,
break your heart?
You saw it from,
the very start.
He says he's kind,
he says it thrice.
You've heard it from,
a dozen guys.
And I still feel,
it all coming down.
He doesn't care,
you're on the ground.
He seemed real kind,
he seemed real nice.
You've heard it from,
one million guys.
And I still feel,
it all coming down.
He doesn't care,
he's never around.
You could die tonight,
he wouldn't move.
You never mattered,
here's the proof.
And I still feel,
it all coming down."

TWINS

The twins perch themselves
On my shoulders and they
Whisper…sweet?...
Something…
To burn or to fade,
They like to debate.
"You should no longer live."
"Well, you never really did."
"The smoke, it's so pretty."
"You're stuck in this city."
I've asked them politely
To please soar away.
No halos in sight.
And they stay.
They stay.

POSSESSED

Anxiety is like
having a haunted house
in your brain.
And the ghosts
are your thoughts.

THAT GOTH GIRL IN MY RELIGION CLASS

Karen dreamed in waves of magenta,
but the nightmares filled her brain
with clouds. She was hanging on
by a wing, but no prayers. Angels
frequently forget about their makers.
Sand fell fast and Karen plotted
to kill her reflection. "I do not like
this woman staring back at me."
We hardly spoke but
I could see right inside:
she had a demon feeding off her
she was trying to hide.
Karen went ghost this one night
last May. The tiger who spent her
time wishing she was endangered
had suddenly gone extinct. No one
understood what happened. But I do.
Karen finally spread her wings and
she flew. Not to heaven…but to
the nearest Joy Division concert.

TOTALED

You're pretty in a car crash kind of way.
I see what's broken, but I want to stay.

VICTORIA

And as I scroll
Your ghost
Reminds me that
You breathe.
I long to scream,
"Hello! Coffee?
Beers?"
But as you
Resurrect
In front of me
I realize
I have nothing
To say to you.
And I never did.

GOODBYE JANET

Oh, oh, Janet.
When you met me,
I wasn't quite aware.
But you had me.
Yes, you had me.
With that stare.

Oh, oh, Janet.
Since you've known me,
We've only been friends.
But I wanted,
Something more.
Something more.

Cause let's have the truth be told.
You're the only one I want to hold.
Girl, I need you like nobody else.
And when you leave, I'll kill myself.

Oh, oh, Janet.
Though I'll miss you,
If only I could kiss you.
Then I wouldn't,
Feel so blue.
Feel so blue.

IF I WERE BETTER LOOKING, WE'D BE SOULMATES

I can't help but think of what we would do,
If only I were as pretty as you.

BON APETIT

we're 60% water and 45% germs,
i shouldn't touch anyone,
but you're too alluring,
as clean as my plate,
i could eat off you
and I'd like to,

THE PEACOCK

The peacock and the benign serpent crawled out of my appendix and made their way through my lower intestine until they burst by the megaphone in waves that shouted marmalade just as red wine manuscripts defenestrated before the altar.

Burp.

EX CETERA

It drives me fucking insane to think
That another man has been with you.
Writing his name in the fresh concrete
That was so clearly mine to vandalize.
I'll crack his skull open with a sledgehammer
And spill his memories of your naked body all over the street.
I'll cut off his organ that you found so much pleasure in
And donate it to the Salvation Army.
I want to murder every lover you've ever had,
They don't deserve to be breathing.
I want to murder every lover you've ever had,

But then I'd have to kill me, too.

…Fine.

PLAY

Sometimes, for fun, I put a gun in my mouth.
Sometimes, for fun, I want to taste bullets.
Sometimes, for fun, I pull the trigger.
Sometimes, for fun, I pull it again.
Sometimes, for fun, I load it.
Sometimes, for fun, I

BUTTERFLYING TO A DINER WITH HEART ON THE MENU

I want to split my heart in two.
I'll keep the smaller half and
give the bigger one to you.
Maybe then you will see,
that you are the only person
motivating it to beat.
I'll probably slowly start to die,
If this small half of mine and a
Large half of yours don't collide.
Every time you even come near,
my chest butterflies and falling
is suddenly not something to fear.
My lungs collapse and I can't taste.
I know my heart is garbage but
don't leave it with your waste.
I'm fragile so please handle with care.
Feast on my heartstrings, they have
more flavor when cooked rare.

EVIL URGES

I fell in love with Elizabeth sometime
last summer during Lollapalooza.
She offered me acid as My Morning
Jacket was intoxicating my eardrums.
Weed was invading my nosedrums
and increasing the quality of real drums.
Her smile told me I would have to respond
"yes." Her eyes were dilated and they
were painfully euphoric. She had red
streaks in her hair, and also in her soul.
Veronica was a unicorn when we met.
She cried silver tears and there might
as well have been a horn bursting
out of her perfect forehead. She donated
money to charities but would tell
her poor sisters to fuck themselves. I
didn't understand her, but I loved her.
She found out about Liz and added breathing
fire to her list of skills. The smell of the fling
outweighed the fumes lingering from the fest.
I fell in love with them when we met,
but I knew I wasn't capable of being
somebody's rock until I had tossed around
a few more stones of my own. Veronica
expected too much, and Liz wanted almost
nothing. The better side of me desired both
women, and the best side of me desired neither.
Last week, a hungry pig called me at work.
Veronica's wings were stripped. She had shot Liz
in the forehead while wearing MY morning jacket.
Circuital.

POEM WITHOUT SHELTER

The rain falls hard but I don't blink.
If words are sparks, then yours are burns.
I drown my feelings in the kitchen sink.
Haven't tasted Sandy in over a week-
her joy was a line I never quite learned.
The rain falls hard but I don't blink.
Sometimes I forget my blood's not ink.
If love's a ride then I skipped my turn.
I drown my feelings in the kitchen sink.
Our chemistry faded; my affection is zinc.
I polluted the stem of the prettiest fern.
The rain falls hard but I don't blink.
I fear brain death but I still think.
A spotless mind is surely what I yearn.
I drown my feelings in the kitchen sink.
Your tongue was a dish I used to eat,
but the heart was a meal I never earned.
The rain falls hard but I don't blink,
I drown my feelings in the kitchen sink.

CONFESSION NO. 27

Today, I will stop eating flesh because
it is too rough for my teeth. I can't chew
through it. Tony Moss sinned again last week
so I baked pieces of his brain into
chocolate chip cookies and ate them for
dessert. I am the next Charlie Trotter.
I can break people, but not my habits.
Killing is wrong but the demon forces
me to drink blood and transform into a
beast I've read no books on. The Bible does
not have advice for those of us who have
already broken all the commandments.
I hate making love and I love to make
hate. It grows in my garden like a rose
with thorns sharp enough to slice through a soul.
The sun does not warm me or help me sprout,
and I remain as cold-blooded as the
snakes that slither through my victims' organs.
My heart pounds as quickly as yours, but I
am as alive as anything you'd dig
up in a cemetery. Those I've touched
no longer breathe, but I do, heavily.
You begin to see the beauty in life
after you take it away so often.

KARLA CHOKED ON HER VOMIT

and I sprayed my carpet down with bleach to kill the germs. Alexandra bought me the guitar Kurt Cobain "played" and then a bus crushed her on her way to get a clit piercing. She should have been a son. I could tell you about how Donnie jumped off a skyscraper and landed inside some wealthy fucker's Ferrari, but that story was all over the news last summer, and I'm sure you've already heard it.

Tyrone's mother poisoned his Lucky Charms after he pawned off her jewelry for coke money, and I had no dealer for a couple months. There was a leprechaun at his wake. Benny opened his veins a week after Tyrone died just so he could be with him in "paradise." I don't know what comes after death, but I doubt my two bisexual, drug addicted, high school friends are dancing on a cloud next to Mother Teresa...

Ashley died and I almost cried because I think I was in love with her. I never told anyone...I thought there would be more time, but cancer spreads a lot quicker than any gossip between my friends. Vernon drowned in Madison's backyard pool during her 21st birthday celebration. That was a buzz kill. We told him it was a bad idea to drink a whole bottle of Jack and then see how long he could his breath, but some people don't listen.

My aunt died the same night as my sister, and something inside of me probably did as well. Stella almost died in a car crash the night we first kissed. She totaled her Toyota and went into a coma. She's not officially dead, but I don't think she'll ever be alive again. Tommy ODed, then Peter was murdered, and then finally, I died. I really don't feel any different...I think I'm as unfazed by my own demise as I am by everyone else's. Cool.

THE TITANIC SINKS SLOWER THAN MY HEART

They say,
"Wake up,"
but I say,
"Why?"
It happened
again; the
Titanic began
to sink.
I was
onboard.
Jackie had
a ticket.
We were
passengers.
Rem was
steering.
I feared
nothing
until Jackie
jumped ship.
So they say,
"Wake up,"
and I say,
"You first."

SPANISH PRINCESS

Speak to me in Spanish and put me in a trance.
I'll taste your spicy lengua at every given chance.
I want your brown eyes on me always, never look away.
You're the first and last thing I see each and every day.
I love your lips, your hair, and the way you say my name.
And if you love me too, my heart is yours to claim.
You've become my muse and the reason I even breathe.
Your gaze and your heart are the only religions I believe.
I'm so lovesick for you, I don't think it's a secret.
This is all I have, so I pray that you will keep it.
You're as gorgeous on the inside as you are on the surface.
And that's what humbles me, I know I don't deserve this.
You're too good for me, it's plain for all to see.
Rico Suave probably wonders why you even waste your time with me.
But I'm glad you do cause I love our conversations.
You're my deepest fantasy, and its manifestation.
You're my Spanish princess and I need you by my side.
If you were to keep my love, you know you'd be my pride.

NINETEEN MILES

Sometimes you forget which brake
you're supposed to be hitting.
I remember drinking at a bar ten
miles south of Milwaukee,
so I wish one of my so-called amigos
could explain to me how I woke
up this morning in St. Paul?
My brain is beating harder
than my heart ever has.
To say this has been a trip
is a severe understatement.
I was in Chicago a mere
twenty-four hours ago,
and I think all my luggage
is now in the hands of the
same vultures who routinely
choose to prey on me.
I'd fall asleep but
I already have.
My drug of choice last
nite must have been every
thing on the menu.
I remember sucking on a
lime to numb the taste
Patron leaves on my tongue.
…And that's about it.
The number of contacts
in my phone seems to have
increased by about four…

so I can only hope that
they are all chicks.
Blacking out is almost
like dreaming your
reality was the dream.
Your nightmares sound
more realistic to you
than what those around
you say actually happened.
Sleep after strong doses
of acid is always a question.
I pinch myself frequently.
The closest restaurant
to my car is already closed.
So, it's a good thing I
can feed off of
frustration about as
well as I can off
of any given meal.
This car smells like
vomit. And I think
the trash bags in my
backseat are the culprits.
This is not
the time to
get pulled over.
When you live in fear,
you already know what
will wet your fuse.
My car is in one piece,
but I certainly am not.
No seatbelt can prepare
for the collision I

will face in Chicago.
I know I'm at the wheel,
but I swear my face
has just gone soaring
through the windshield.

SEAWEED

Nothing tastes better on the outside than it does
At the bottom of the ocean
You're tied to the anchor and you're quickly descending
Lavish times long past lay in your brain
Like the termites you forgot to evict
The joke in it all is that time is bleeding
And you can feel its grip on your ankle
The spark was lit when you had something to give
But the wind would never let it spread
It's amazing what one will do
To get a taste of nothing
Sometimes I feel as if I'm drowning
Before I've even touched the water

AMELIE, JE T'AIME

Amelie ends the film happy,
But I don't.
She finally meets the only man her heart flutters for.
But I'm convinced that he was not made for her like I am.
"She doesn't relate to other people,
She was always a lonely child,"
Amelie says about herself.
"But you relate to me,"
I want to tell her,
"And I'm just as lonely as you. We're…destined for one another."
But then I remember that she's not real,
And my longing for her will never be reciprocated.
They say a woman without love wilts like a flower without sun.
Well I'm a man.
And I've never even felt daylight.

LIMBO

Well, bottle of tequila in hand,
This wasn't what he had planned.
The ragtime felt like a drag.
He felt his body quake,
And the shotty's shake.
Left that night in a bag.

TWO MASKS

Two masks were made in the dark one day,
In the town of St. Petersburg was where they'd stay.
They were drafted and chiseled and steamed to perfection,
So, they became their maker's only source of affection.
He cherished them and they never left his sight,
Until a thief stole them one cold July night.
He searched and searched but he made no connection,
And he slowly grew to despise his reflection.
His sanity now gone just like his masks,
The crafter decided to pick up an axe.
He smashed in his floorboards and cut off his legs,
Bled to death, and left a note on his bed.
Young Charlotte Brown of Atlanta, Georgia,
Happened across them on a harsh August scorcher.
She put one on and that's all she needed,
It attached to her face and the copper just heated.
She now resides in a cottage near Maine,
Those masks, I tell you, drove the poor girl insane.

JACKIE

I picked up cigarettes to impress you,
and now I'm addicted.

EXTRACURRICULAR

I think if I killed myself, I'd do it at my college's student center. Maybe then, the boys would know my name and the girls would shriek for me. They'd put their smart phones down for a beat, point at the bloody pieces of my skull, and remark, "ha, I guess he finally opened up."

Can't blame 'em.

BUMBLE

I just spent two dollars on something called fucking "Bumble coins" just to "super" swipe somebody on this shallow ass dating app and I'm pretty sure this is the low point of my life. Just send somebody to fucking kill me now, it can't get worse than this.

...But also, maybe pray she swipes back first? Eh. Fuck it. Kill, then pray. More poetic. Happy Thursday. I need sleep.

THERE ONCE WAS A MAN

There once was a man,
He lived in a small town.
The man saw cats,
Cats with tiny paws.
The man didn't like the cats,
Or the paws.
The man bought a cat.
The man owned a razorblade.
The man had an idea.
The cats didn't bother him as much anymore.

MAMMOTH

No one seems to notice there's a mammoth in the room,
Despite how loud the poor girl cries.
The saddest part is that it happened so soon,
Before the two had real goodbyes.
This girl was everything the boy had dreamed,
But there was a clear issue from the start.
He loved her but it wasn't as it seemed.
She no longer wanted his heart.
Conversation wore thin and so did he,
He only longed for her.
The girl told him she was always busy,
And he didn't want to bore her.
If they hadn't before they surely noticed now,
The mammoth had taken flight, and slowly started to howl.

VILLANELLE FOR MY BELLE

Her face stains my brain like juice stains a rug.
And though I already know she likely will not,
She's the only woman I want to feel my love.

I turned wine red when she only gave me a hug.
I could feel my lips begging hers to unlock.
Her face stains my brain like juice stains a rug.

I pray every night to the big guy above.
Hoping that her cold will stop.
She's the only woman I want to feel my love.

She's a garden and I'm the hungry bug.
I'd only pollute her if I touched her crops.
Her face stains my brain like juice stains a rug.

I dream often but truth wakes me with a shove.
Time once stood but now it simply blocks.
She's the only woman I want to feel my love.

I'm too deep to climb out of this hole I've dug,
I've buried myself and I haven't access to a clock.
Her face stains my brain like juice stains a rug.
She's the only woman I want to feel my love.

BLACK

Wash over my eyes and eat my flesh,
The time is up and I've failed the test.
I want to take a blade and run it down my arm.
When I see I bleed black, I won't be alarmed.
I know I'm empty inside, apart from the organs.
They're victims of neglect, for I often ignore them.
Strange how this destruction of my lungs and my liver,
Seems to be the only gift life has to deliver.
We're all black deep down but few really know it,
And we think others are crazy when they finally show it.

Giving up the ghost is tempting; I know he wants out.
I flirt with the next world just to see what'll sprout.
Don't think this one is working, there's too much pain.
I think the only way out is to pop my veins.
There once was a light, but the tunnel's gotten darker.
There's not even enough fire to light up a sparkler.
We're all doomed to see the truth for ourselves.
You only have "you," there's no one else.
One day we'll all open up, there will be no going back.
Watch as the streets are devoured by a long sea of black.

MADELINE'S FACE

I swear the mask was made sometime last May,
the summer she carved Mark into her thigh.
The two changed together like night and day,
she bought matching coffins in case they died.

Maddie soon painted her nails with magenta,
as her blood melted to a shade of black.
Hell grew inside her near the placenta,
slowly waiting for its time to attack.

Mark alone couldn't quench her newest thirst,
and she decided she needed a tan.
When designer brands could no longer work,
Maddie gagged on the one in her van.

Maddie's complexion is truly a waste,
for the mask smiles where she once had a face.

90 DOWN DAKIN

I'm going 90 down Dakin and I just cut my brakes.
I know I'm only human, but I got what it takes.
If I crash, I won't die, the adrenaline assures.
I've never followed rules and I guess that's my curse.
The smoke and the smell will make me feel whole.
What my future holds, I don't want to know.
You're like a bandit with the way you snatched my heart.
And you're probably the reason I crash all my cars.

105 DEGREES

I'm so lovesick, and for who?
Catch the love bug like I catch the flu.
Three days on the mend and then I'm cured.
Soaring high, feeling like a bird.
But I hit the gravel when you cross my path.
Me + You = Bliss, I've done the Math.
But you aren't so willing to be in the equation.
Despite what I do, you resist my persuasion.
1 is lonely, and so am I.
Doomed to be odd no matter what I try.
One day you'll wake up, you'll smell the hoses.
Long after I've fallen victim to lethal love doses.

VERONICA

Because, Veronica's smile, it lit the world.
And now I can't look at any other girl.
What can I say? I need Veronica by my side.
What can I do? I wish you never left that night.
So cruel.

She was once was my queen, but I broke her crown.
And now my renegade doesn't want me around.
What can I say? I need Veronica by my side.
What can I do? I wish you never left that night.
Ooh, ooh.

And I'm sorry that you think, we aren't meant to be.
I gave you everything, and you had no empathy.
Now, after all this time, you've come back to my city.
Please turn back now, we're done showing you pity.

Because, Veronica's smile, it lit the world.
And now I can't look at any other girl.
What can I say? I need Veronica by my side.
What can I do? I wish you never left that night.
So cruel.

Fuck.

PAVEMENT

This is my mouth chewing concrete under your stiletto.

You look good from this angle.

NO VACANCY

You still wanna make it work,
But there is no vacancy.
You're a clever kinda girl,
What is it you can't see?
Until you find the time to grow,
Where you're concerned,
My heart is full.

THE LAST (COVID THOUGHTS)

It's almost 6 am and I still haven't slept because all I can do is lie in bed and think. Because what else is there to do during quarantine but think? About everything. But mostly - who I was before this began, all the plans I had for myself, everything I was looking forward to, and everything I was dreading.

And the last time...So many last times that were impossible to recognize: The last time I saw them, the last time I went there, the last time I did this, the last time I felt that, the last time I touched her...Some things will return. Maybe by July or August. 2021 or 2022. But some never will. And I wish I could have appreciated them. I would have grabbed them and held them and squeezed them with every inch of strength I've forever been afraid to show another human being...

I'd like to say this is the last time I'll have these thoughts. But I can't. Just like me, they have nowhere else to go.

JERI'S GRILL

The clock doesn't move here
And neither do we
Why get a wife when
My waitress knows exactly what I like
The coffee is always hot
And the customers are always cold
I like my toast the way I like my commute
Everything's better with some jam
If you'd have told me this booth was my coffin
I'd have ordered another short stack
Better the smell of burnt eggs
Than embalming fluid

SLEEP

Every time I have a nightmare,
I wake up with an erection.

TRUMP

Fat
Idiot
Asshole

Tweet this

#kissmyass

BEND 'ER

If this hangover were the only proof of
Our time together I'd ever have,
I'd gladly sweat it out
Forever.

SOUTH

All this time
I thought
I could fly
But now I see
I never even
Had wings

BUBBLEGUM

Sometimes I forget I'm an ant until I see the foot coming down on me.

BEATLE

I'd hold your hand
But it would only make your palms bleed.

GIN

Eventually life itself
becomes one long drunken night.
You remember a bit of the good
and a bit of the bad,
but most of it is just a blur.
Of course, you eventually black out,
and try as you might,
the next day is Hell.

ICEBREAKER

Sometimes I think
If I could meet a woman
Who hates me
As Much as I
Hate myself
I'd have found
My soulmate.
And if I could find
Someone who loves me
As much as I love myself
We wouldn't talk.

Want another drink?

VOYAGER

I'd like to be a
Stranger again and
Travel somewhere far
Tell them all
I've mattered once
And someone would
Believe it

FRIENDLY FIRE

I can count on me
to ruin every
good thing I have
going for myself
and at the end of the day
no one fucks
me harder
than myself

SCROLL

I used to believe
Every word mattered
But now it's clear
Nobody's reading.

CARNIVALE

No one leaves and I like it that way.
The sky isn't even half dark.
Sharon said that you called her again.
And Lionel wants his turn.
I've dreamt of winning that Green Day poster.
But today kind of feels maroon.
So, when Mark and I puke at the gate.
It has nothing to do with the burgers.
She tastes like cotton candy.
But my dentist says it'll ruin my teeth.
When we reach the top of the carousel.
I'll be sure to have mistletoe.
I know it says the month's July.
But I think I feel a draft.
I wish that I could actually aim.
But I never shoot out the star.
Next year, there is…always next year.
Will you settle for a goldfish?

FLOATERS

you're like the sun
you're so beautiful
from afar
but as I get closer
you just really start
to hurt my eyes

TRIMESTER

Time heals all wombs
Except for the one
That gave way to you

290 CHARACTERS OR LESS

Why does the brain that brings me so much joy, so much creativity, and so much inspiration also have to be the brain that gives me so much anxiety, sadness, and self-hate? Like, if you bought a Ferrari and it ran great most the time, but a few days out of the month the steering wheel just decided to guide you towards a brick wall…you'd return it, no?

PUPA

I have spent the last five years
Thinking it was physically impossible
For anyone to stir sleeping butterflies
Inside my stomach again.
But this past week has shown
There's a larva that hums.
And even if it never soars again,
I'm just glad to know it could.

STAND

I've fallen in love again.
The face I won't forget
Hangs on my mantle
Until tomorrow.

150/90

The things you love
End up killing you
Cherish them now
Before you cut them from your diet.

DOCTOR

Doctor,
There's this weird thing
Beating inside my chest.
I'm told it's normal
But I've never
Felt like this before.
I know it's costly,
I know it stings,
But I have insurance.
So, please, pretty please,
Do you think you can remove it?

TINDER BIO

I'm not afraid of
Getting my heart broken
Again.
I'm afraid my heart
Can't be broken
Again.

FERAL ROSE

Sometimes my life feels like the last paragraph of an early chapter of a really long book. I like this sentence, but if I keep rereading it forever, I'll never know how good the story is. It's time to turn the page.

CEREMONIAL

If you've ever left your own party
And watched the revelers carry on
I think you already know
What happens when we die

YOUR RED DRESS

The Beatles had it right
Don't wear red tonight
To you it's just a show
But I'll become a bull
We can't let the patrons view
As I rip it off of you

BEAUTY MARKS

I want to kiss
Every
Spot
Blemish
Freckle
Bruise
Mole
And
Scar
Present on
Your Skin.
Funny how
Your “flaws”
Only make
You more
Perfect.

JEWEL-OSCO

I am not a birthday cake.
I cannot cut myself
Into even pieces
And share them with
Everyone who needs a wish.

KRYSTAL SAVES THE DAY

I think it's important to have something that makes your heart skip beats, whether it's a memory, a job, a pet, a place, or a person…

Not all palpitations hint towards our demise; some tell us we're alive.

ARTSY GIRL

Artsy girl, you have me
You don't even have to try
Put me in a painting and
Dip your brush into my eye
I want to be your only muse
You'll write lyrics to my voice
Lie with me and watch your films
Let's drown all outside noise
Show me all that you create
As we shout each other's names
That passion for the work you make
Turns my thoughts soon into flames
Artsy girl, you have me
You don't even have to try
Put me in a painting and
I'll put you in mine

THE GHOST OF LINCOLN AVENUE

Lawrence.
Irving.
Belmont.
Fullerton.
I cross them all
And no one sees me
I like it that way
I pass holding hands
And happy humans
But I'm never one
I like it that way
The Christmas lights
Remind me
Of how romantic
This whole season is
And could be
But no one sees me
And I like it that way?
Armitage.

STARKIST

The starkest tuna fish lives forever but I don’t.

W8T1N

A text from you
Does more than
Light up my phone
It lights up
My soul

DINGBAT SIDEKICK

I dreamt about
The most beautiful girl
I've ever seen
And then I
Woke up
Next to her.
When I'm with you,
I truly am
Living the dream.

WITHOUT YOU

Absence makes the heart grow fonder,
But being without you makes the day feel longer.

OSTRICH

Today I wish I
Were an Ostrich.
Better to dig my face
So far underground
That everybody thinks
I'm dead,
Than to ever let
Anyone think
I'm alive again.

DOVE

If I sent you away
In search of love,
Would you come
Flying back
To us?
My ark may hold
Only one of me,
But I don't need two,
I just need you.

HEAVENSENT

Sometimes in life
You're blessed with
Meeting an angel.
And just cause you
Play with their halos
Doesn't mean
You're a demon.
But it also doesn't mean
You aren't.

YOU ARE SO MUCH MORE THAN AN ANT

You are so much more than an ant
Despite all the feet you see up above
If only they knew how strong you are
Who else can carry ten times their weight?
You may feel small, but to me, you aren't
And together, we'll topple them all

STARS

Baby,
When I look at the stars,
You're what I see.
Why make a wish
When you're already
With me?

TWO SKELETONS

They say we're nothing more
Than bones and meat and flesh
But I know that isn't true
Each time I taste your breath
For so long, I was told I'd die
Before meeting my other half
The joke's on them, I now see
Why cry when I can laugh?
My hand was made to hold yours
And yours made to fit mine
Now that I see you walk this earth
I can't waste no more time
When I kiss you, I feel
My heart begin to scream
But not in pain, nor not in fear
It's found its one true dream
I know our meeting was destined
I've never been more certain
It can be hard to contain how good I feel
But believe me I am learning
We joke and say "two skeletons"
A reference we both find great
But the truth is that we're two bright souls
And this one's found its mate.

WHEN I'M WITH YOU

Let's go for a walk and grab a drink
Tell me all about your day
You clear all clouds inside my head
Make me know things will be okay
When I hold your hand, my heart skips
To our favorite Coldplay songs
An hour has never felt so short
My smile has never felt so long
Big heart, big brain all adorning
The Very best woman I know
I'm not always the man I should be
But you make me want to grow
You water me without realizing
By your laughter and life support
This plant was dying before we met
But now its vines all soar
Zoo Lights, sushi, Scrabble, New Years,
Blood moons, tacos, pigs, and our cheers
Have all made me feel so much better
Than anything I've ever tried
You're my baby and when I'm with you
I know everything feels right.

THE LIFEGUARD

The lifeguard sat,
and watched us all.
Everyone breathes,
but who says we can swim?

www.ingramcontent.com/pod-product-compliance
Lightning Source LLC
Chambersburg PA
CBHW022200160726
48282CB00024B/268
9789390601462